Black Magic White Noise

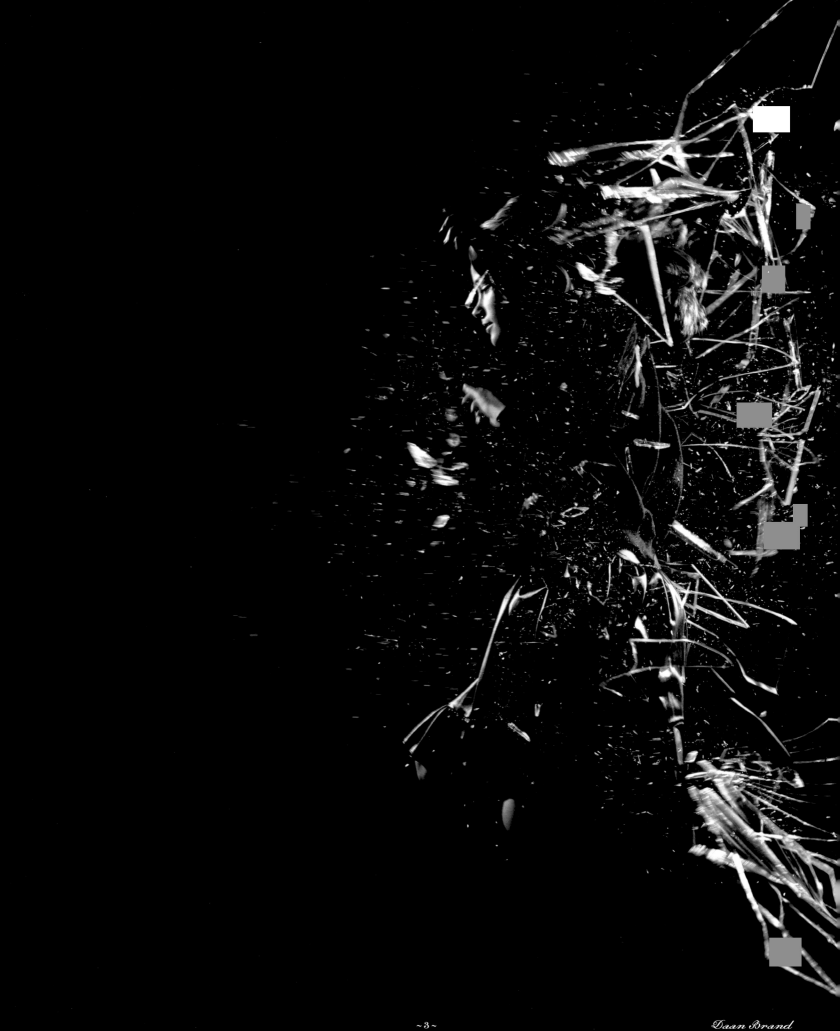

Daan Brand

Daan Brand

Bernd Preiml

Bernd Preiml

Bernd Preiml

Bernd Preiml

Billy & Hells

Billy & Hells

Bernd Preiml

Chris Anthony

Mikko Rantanen

Mikko Rantanen

Mikko Rantanen

Mikko Rantanen

Ben Beirens

Chiharu Shiota

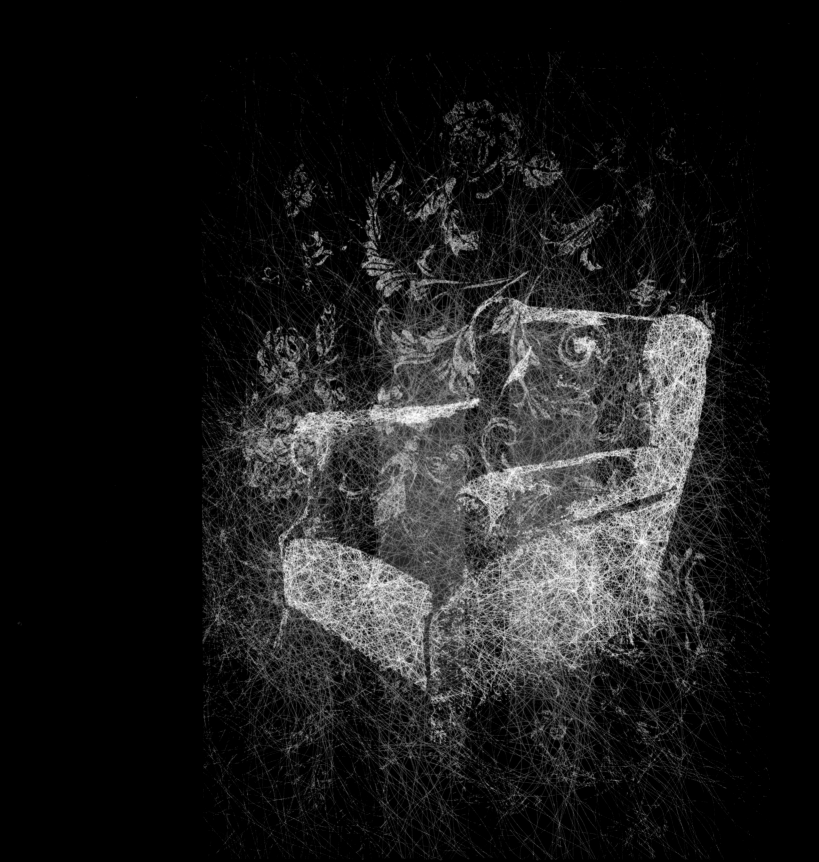

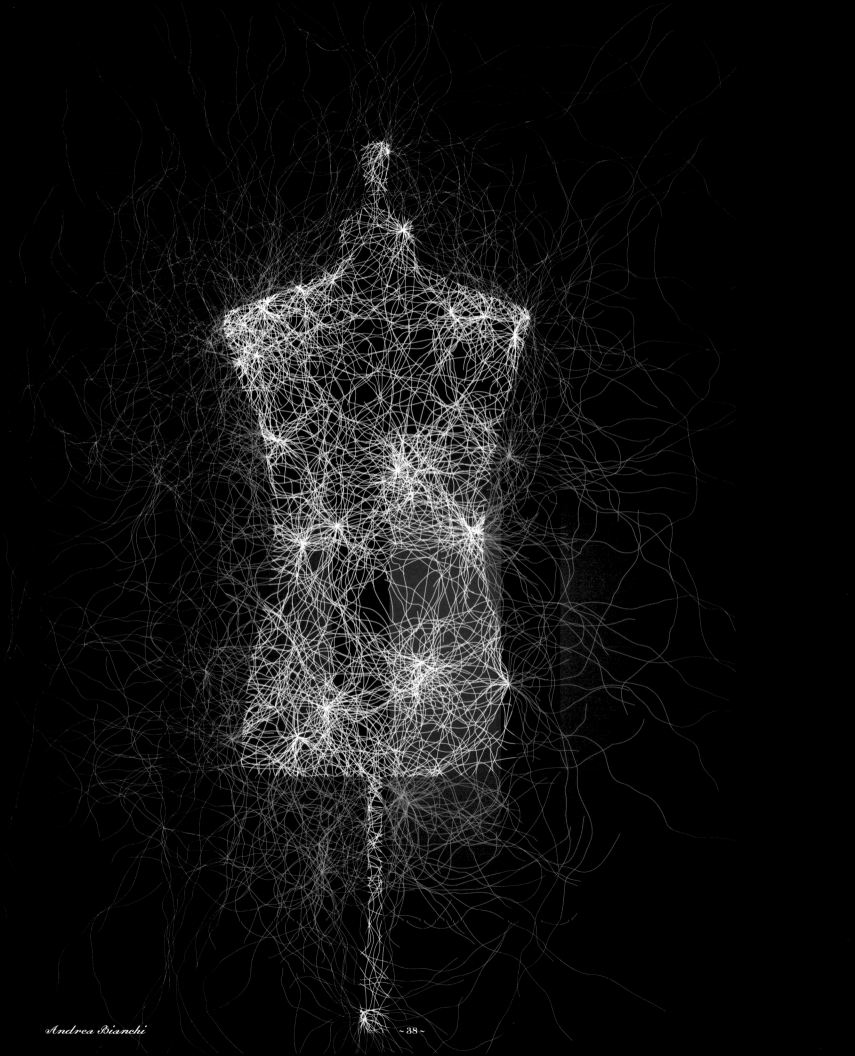

Andrea Bianchi

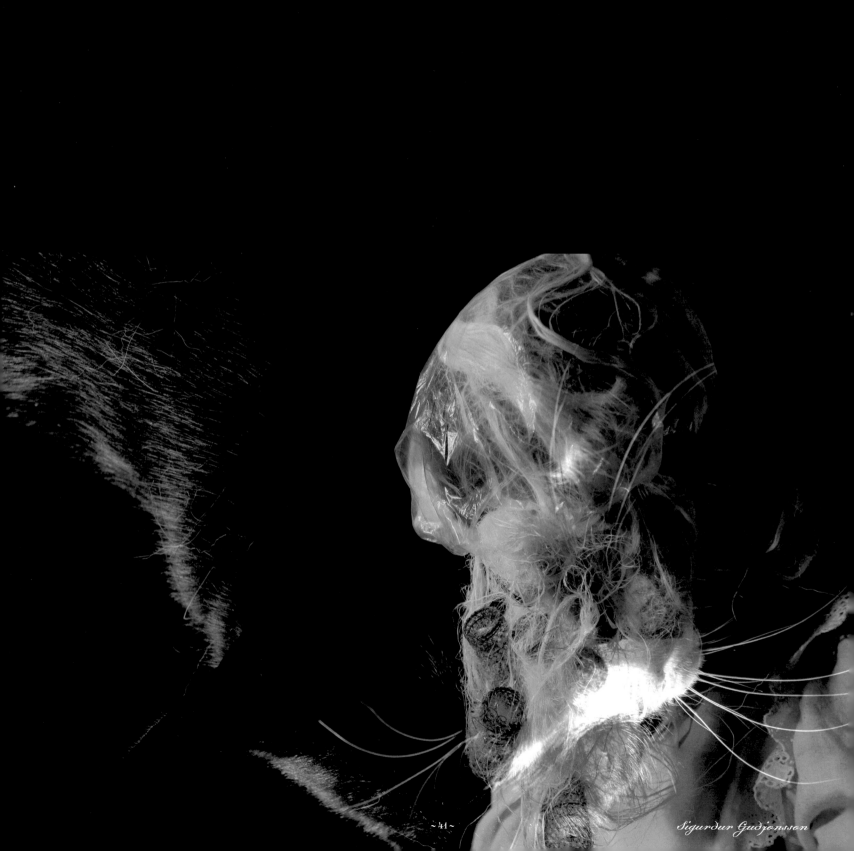

Sigurdur Gudjonsson

Sigurdur Gudjonsson

Liese Lotte

Peter Peiler

Peter Peiler

Léopold Rabus

Léopold Rabus

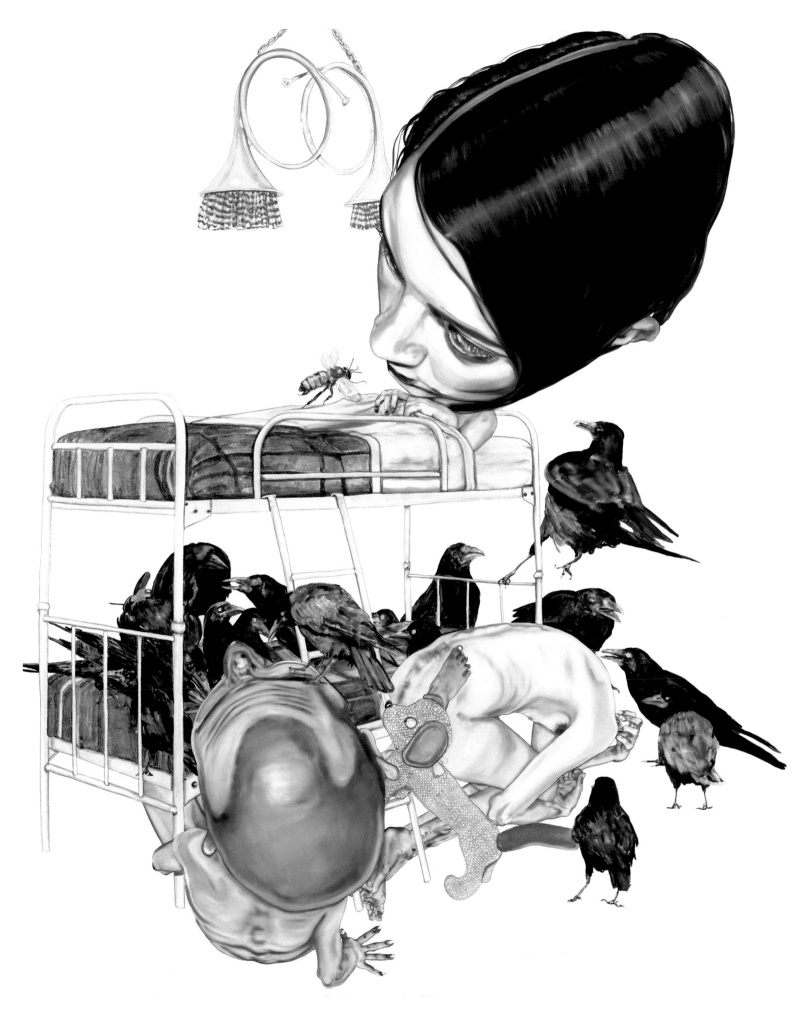

Léopold Rabus

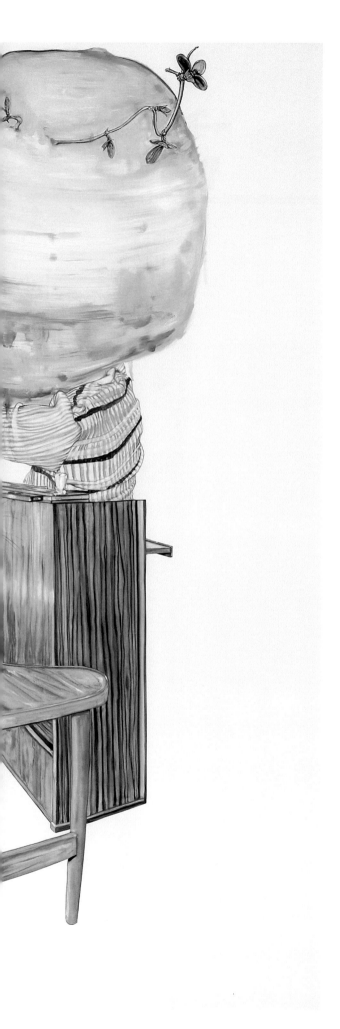

Paul Bakker

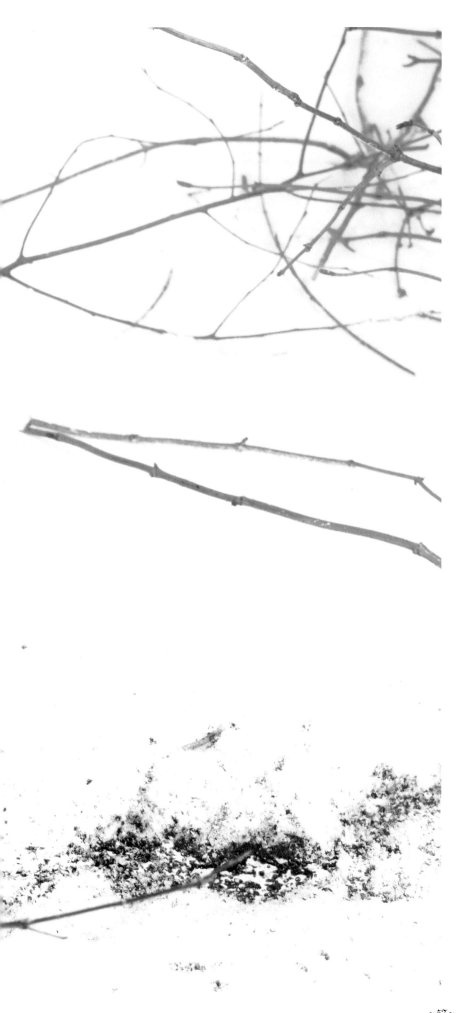

Erwin Olaf

Anne Wenzel

Erick Swenson

CON-
FES-
SION

CATALOG · TK72
ARTIST BLEEDING THROUGH
ALBUM TITLE THE TRUTH
COMPLETE UPC · 824953007226

trustkill

David Black

Dennis Rudolph

Kristian Kozul

Marc Bijl

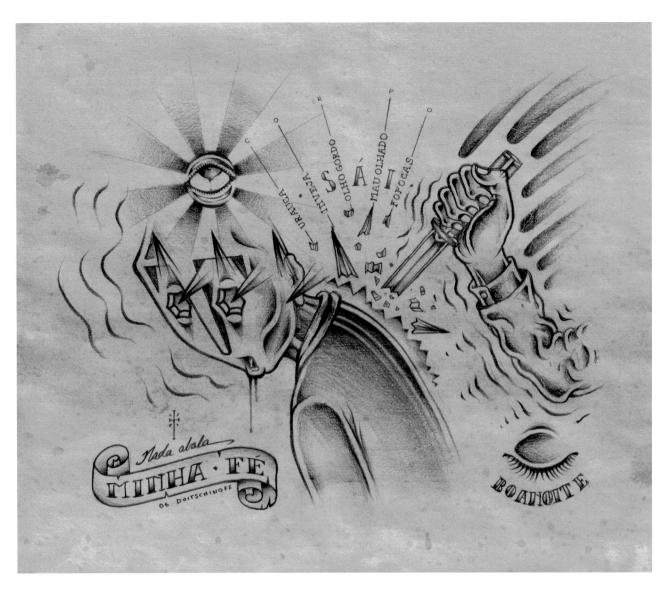

Stephan Doitschinoff

CAPVT COR
VI·PVTREF
FACTIO P
HILOSOPHORVM

Stephan Doitschinoff

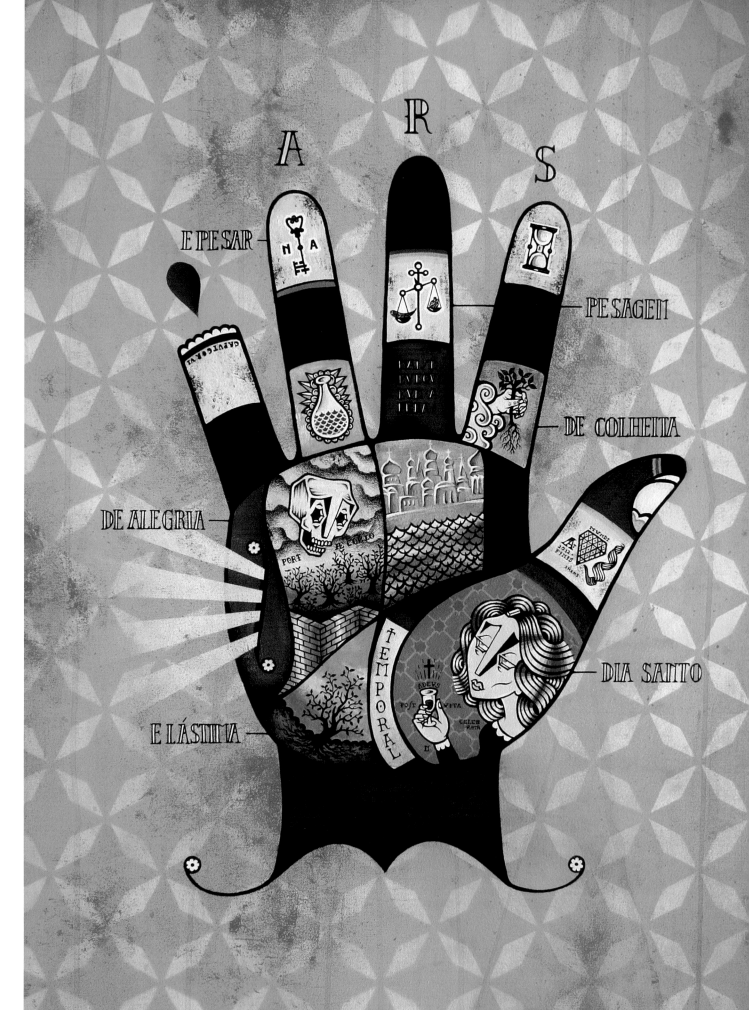

Francesco D'Isa

Francesco D'Isa

Francesco D'Isa

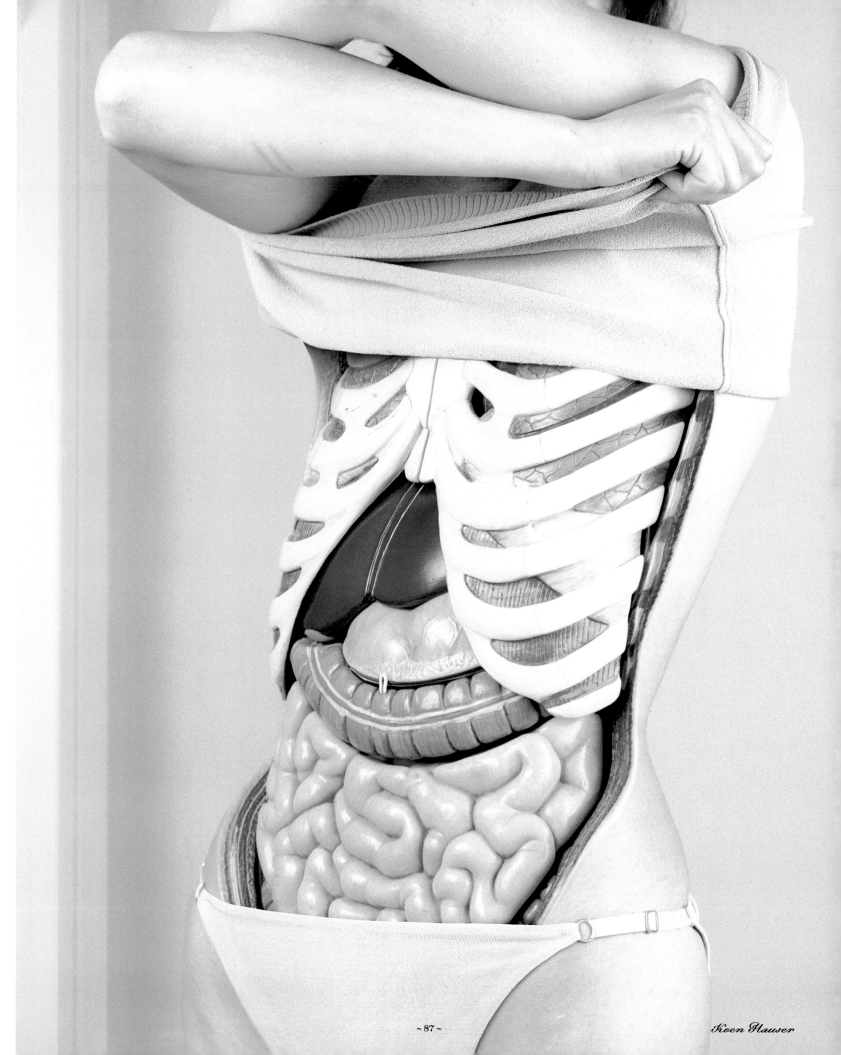

Koen Hauser

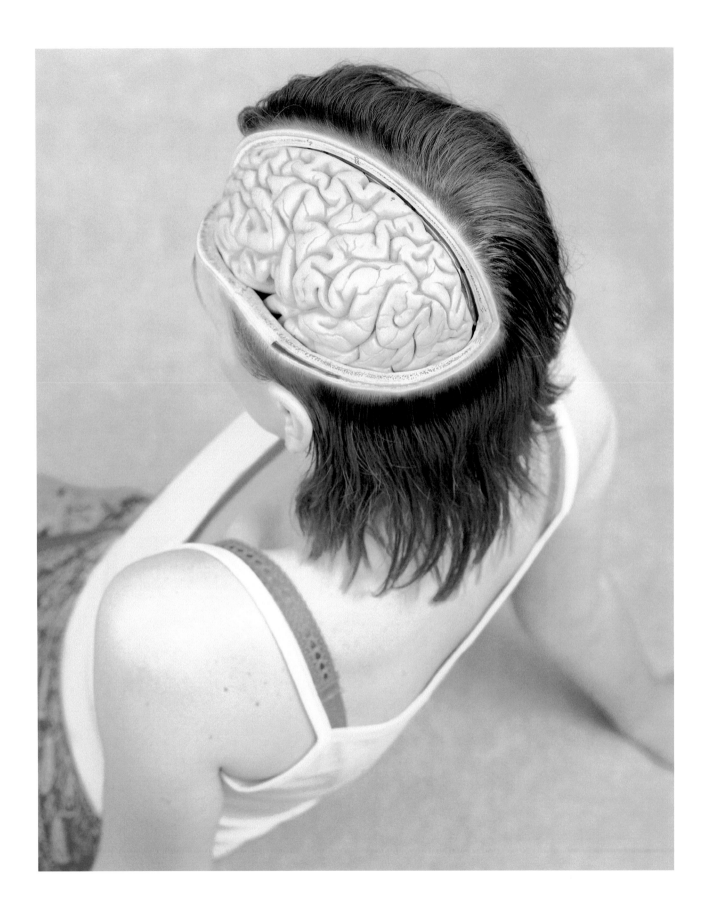

Koen Hauser

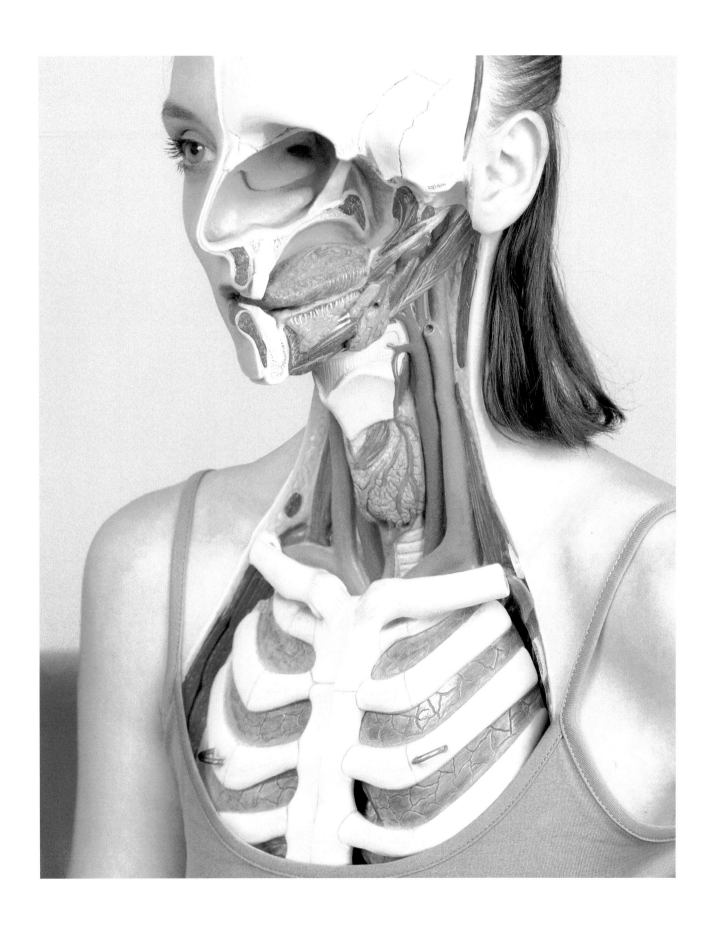

Koen Hauser

Laura Weider

Simen Johan

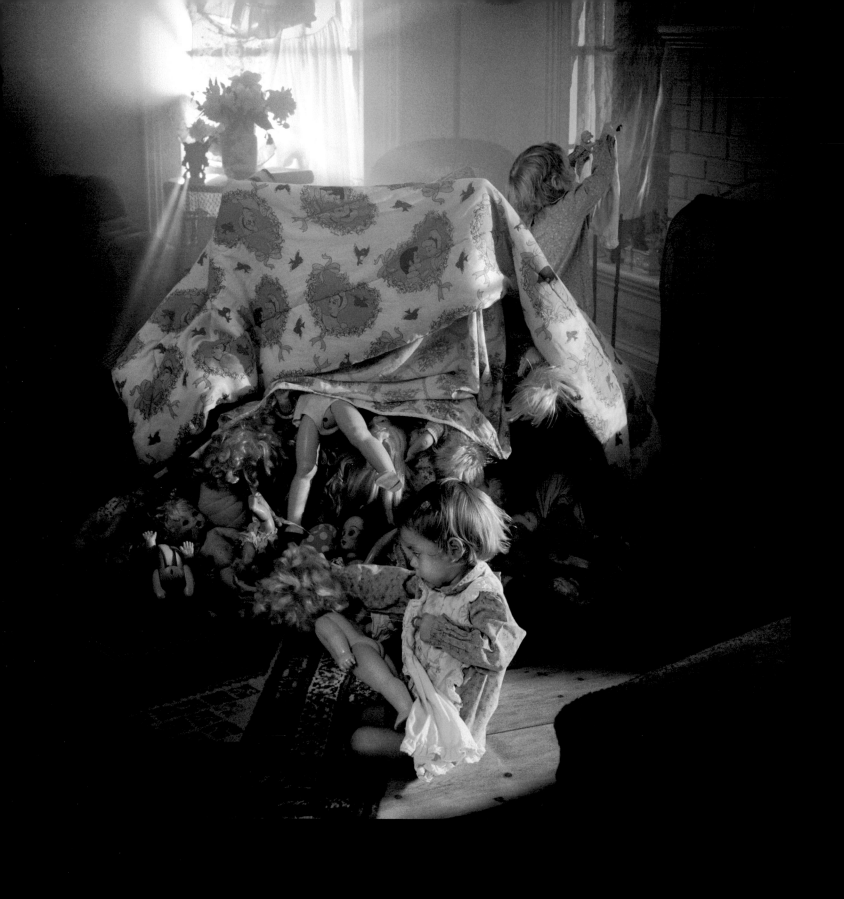

Tessa Farmer

Tessa Farmer

Vania

Vania

Hendrik Haase

Aya Kato

James Dignan

James Dignan

James Dignan

Liese Lotte

Laura Weider

Pathali Schön

Sebastian Assaf

Andrea Bianchi

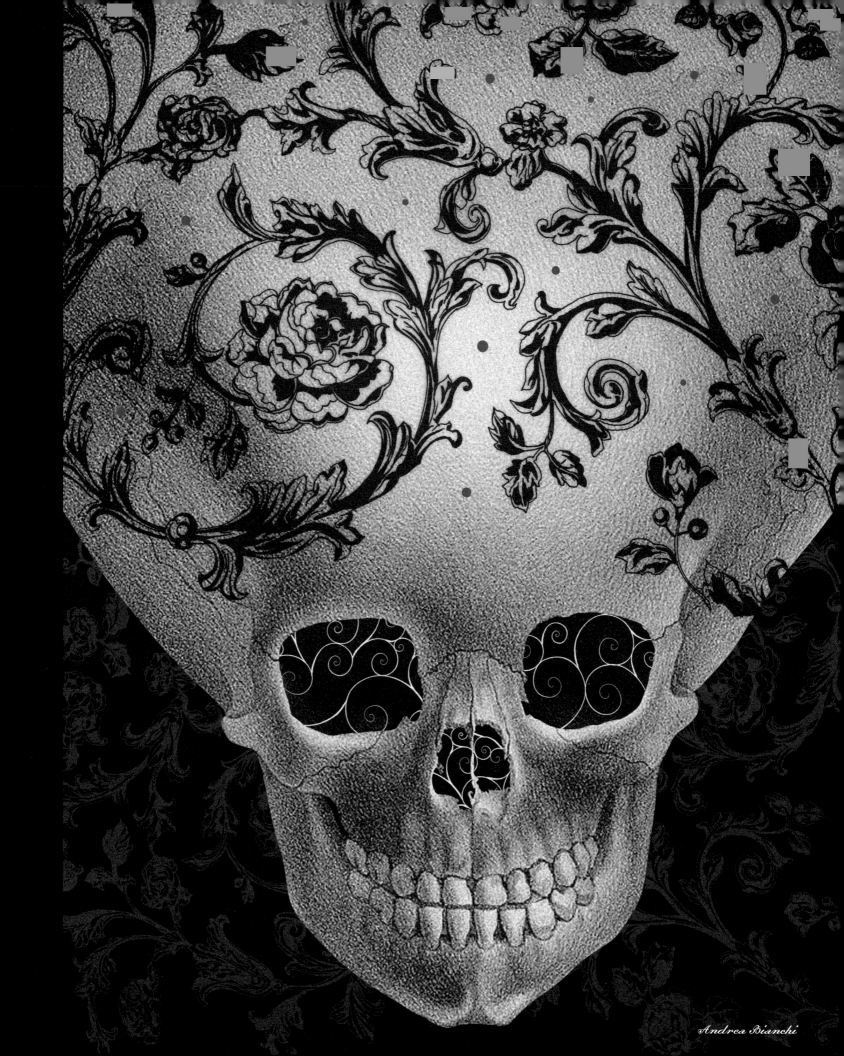

Andrea Bianchi

Andrea Bianchi

Claudia Drake

Joe Biel

Joe Biel

Invisible Creature

Plaseebo

Bernd Preiml

Bernd Preiml

Bernd Preiml

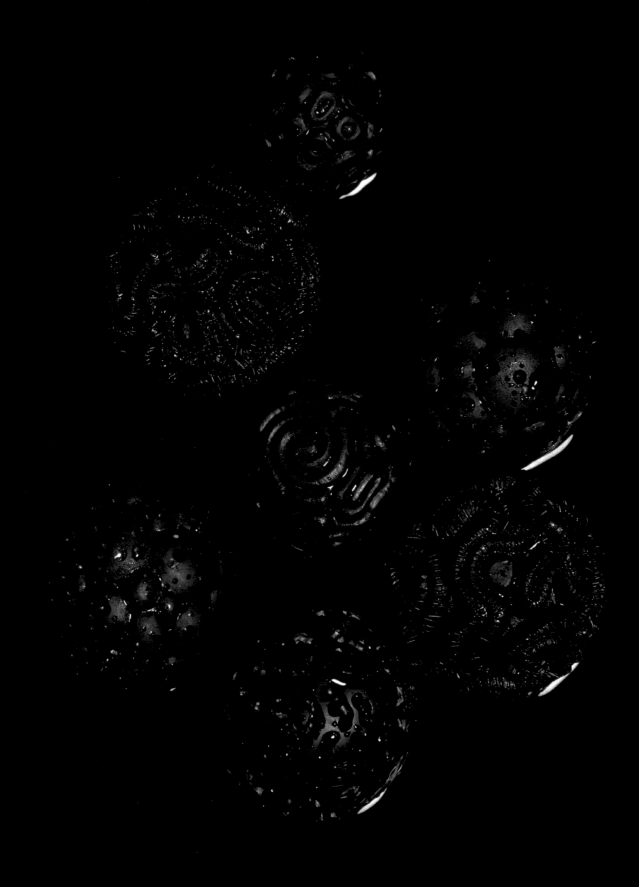

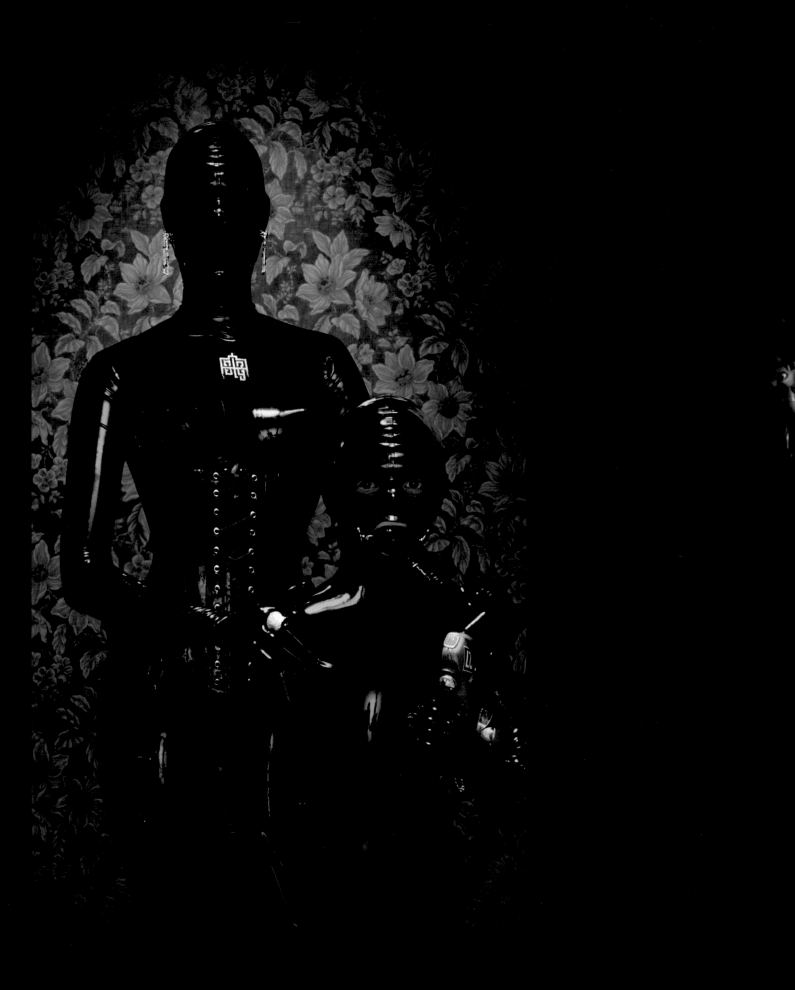

Erwin Olaf

David Black

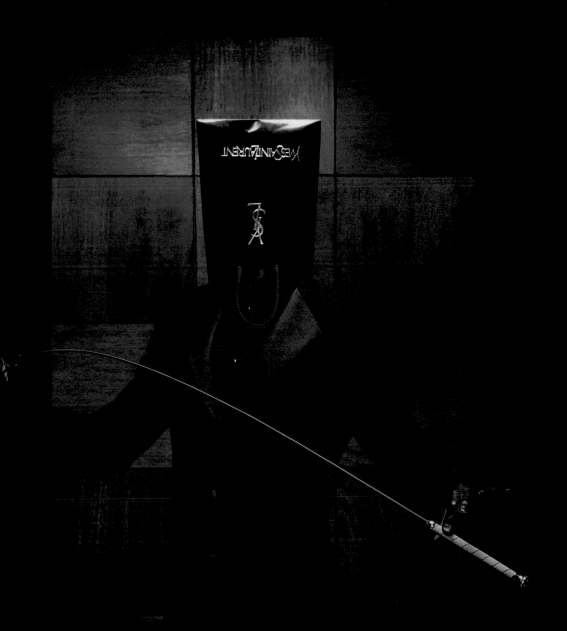

Erwin Olaf

Erwin Blumenfeld

Erwin Olaf

Erwin Olaf

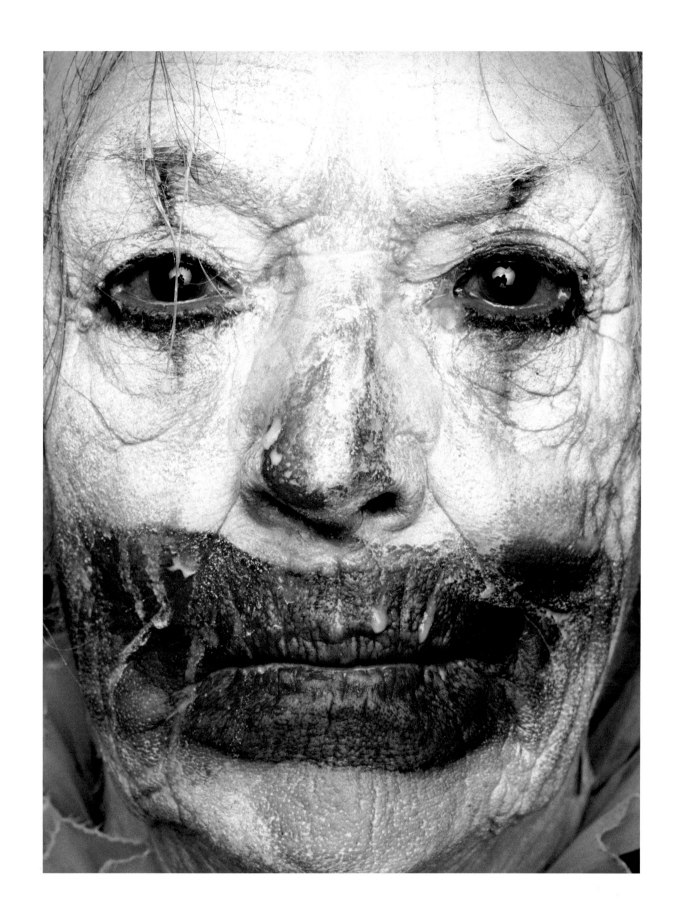

Ervin Olaf

Black Magic, White Noise

Edited by Robert Klanten, Hendrik Hellige, Sven Ehmann

Project management: Hendrik Hellige for dgv
Cover photo: Olff Appold, www.olffappold.com
Layout & design: Birga Meyer for dgv
Production management: Martin Bretschneider for dgv

Printed by fgb – Freiburger Graphische Betriebe GmbH & Co. KG, Freiburg

Published by Die Gestalten Verlag, Berlin 2007
ISBN: 978-3-89955-187-7

Bibliographic information published by the Deutsche Nationalbibliothek.
The Deutsche Nationalbibliothek lists this publication in the Deutsche Nationalbibliografie;
detailed bibliographic data is available on the Internet at http://dnb.d-nb.de.

For more information please check: www.die-gestalten.de

None of the content in this book was published in exchange for payment by commercial
parties or designers; dgv selected all included work based solely on its artistic merit.

Respect copyright, encourage creativity!